AMERICAN PRESIDENTS

George W. Bush

by Rachel Grack

BLASTOFF!
READERS
2

BELLWETHER MEDIA • MINNEAPOLIS, MN

Blastoff! Readers are carefully developed by literacy experts to build reading stamina and move students toward fluency by combining standards-based content with developmentally appropriate text.

Level 1 provides the most support through repetition of high-frequency words, light text, predictable sentence patterns, and strong visual support.

Level 2 offers early readers a bit more challenge through varied sentences, increased text load, and text-supportive special features.

Level 3 advances early-fluent readers toward fluency through increased text load, less reliance on photos, advancing concepts, longer sentences, and more complex special features.

★ **Blastoff! Universe**

Reading Level

Grade
K

Grades
1–3

Grade
4

This edition first published in 2022 by Bellwether Media, Inc.

No part of this publication may be reproduced in whole or in part without written permission of the publisher. For information regarding permission, write to Bellwether Media, Inc., Attention: Permissions Department, 6012 Blue Circle Drive, Minnetonka, MN 55343.

Library of Congress Cataloging-in-Publication Data

Names: Pettiford, Rebecca, author.
Title: George W. Bush / by Rebecca Pettiford.
Description: Minneapolis, MN : Bellwether Media, Inc., 2022. | Series: Blastoff! Readers: American Presidents | Includes bibliographical references and index. | Audience: Ages 5-8 | Audience: Grades 2-3 | Summary: "Relevant images match informative text in this introduction to George W. Bush. Intended for students in kindergarten through third grade"-- Provided by publisher.
Identifiers: LCCN 2021011389 (print) | LCCN 2021011390 (ebook) | ISBN 9781644875148 (library binding) | ISBN 9781648344824 (paperback) | ISBN 9781648344220 (ebook)
Subjects: LCSH: Bush, George W. (George Walker), 1946---Juvenile literature. | Presidents--United States-- Biography--Juvenile literature. | United States--Politics and government--2001-2009--Juvenile literature.
Classification: LCC E903 .P48 2022 (print) | LCC E903 (ebook) | DDC 973.931092--dc23
LC record available at https://lccn.loc.gov/2021011389
LC ebook record available at https://lccn.loc.gov/2021011390

Editor: Elizabeth Neuenfeldt   Designer: Josh Brink

Printed in the United States of America, North Mankato, MN.

Table of Contents

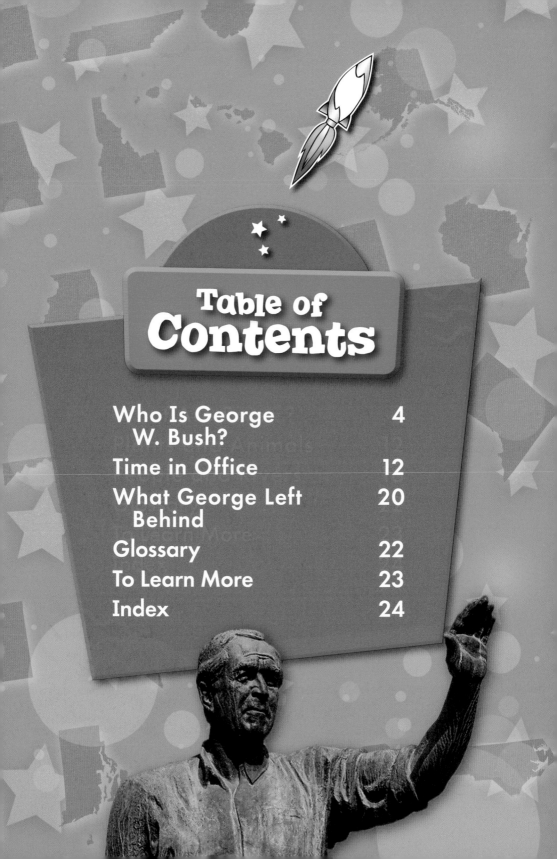

Who Is George W. Bush?   4

Time in Office   12

What George Left Behind   20

Glossary   22

To Learn More   23

Index   24

Who Is George W. Bush?

George. W. Bush was the 43rd president of the United States. He served from 2001 to 2009.

George was president during **9/11**.

George was born in
Connecticut in 1946.
He grew up in Texas.

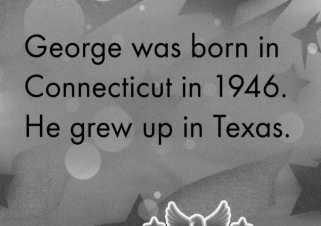

George's Hometown

Midland,
Texas

N
W   E
S

New Haven,
Connecticut

6

George H. W. Bush was his father. He was the 41st president!

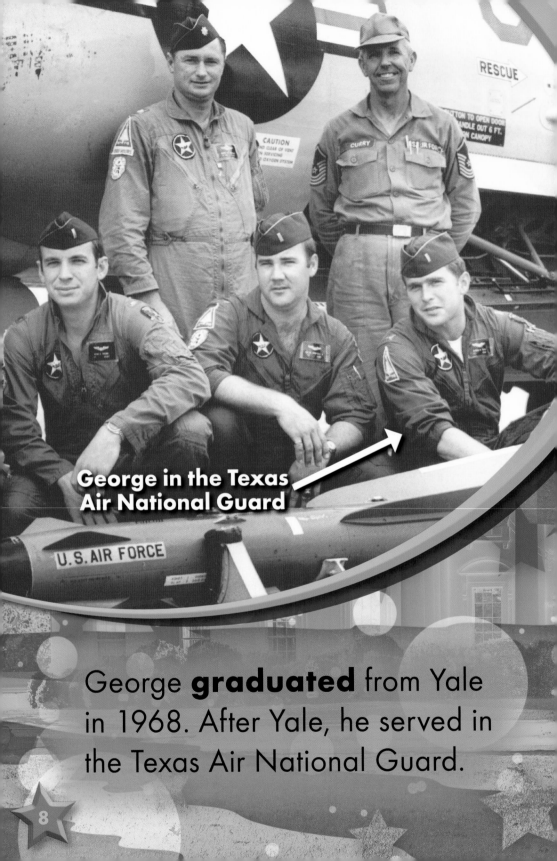

George in the Texas Air National Guard

U.S. AIR FORCE

George **graduated** from Yale in 1968. After Yale, he served in the Texas Air National Guard.

In 1973, George studied at Harvard.

Presidential Picks

Movie

Field of Dreams

Sport

baseball

Food

cheeseburger pizza

Hobby

biking

Afterwards, George started an oil business. He also owned a baseball team!

George was **elected** Texas **governor** in 1994.

11

George ran for president in 2000. He ran against Al Gore.

The election was close.
But George won!

Presidential Profile

Place of Birth

New Haven, Connecticut

Birthday

July 6, 1946

Schooling

Yale University and
Harvard University

Term

2001 to 2009

Party

Republican

Signature

Vice President

Dick Cheney

Months after George became president, 9/11 happened. Many people died.

9/11 attack in New York

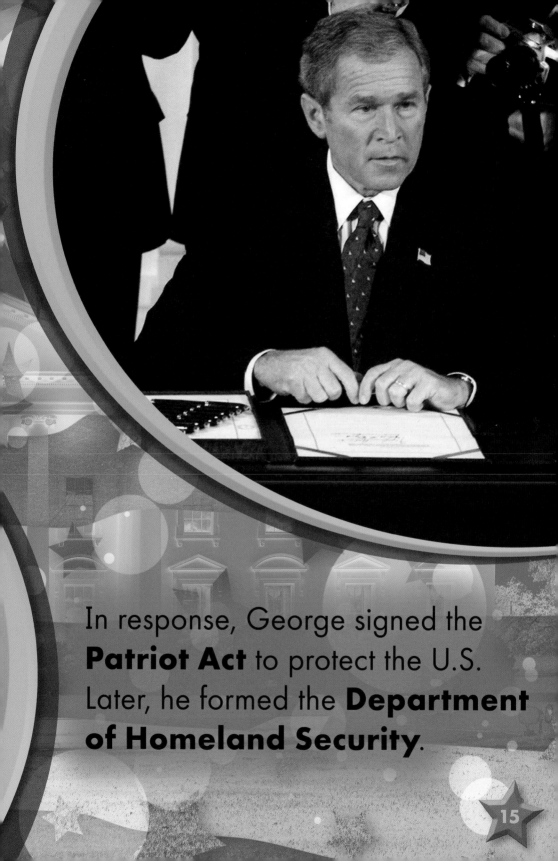

In response, George signed the **Patriot Act** to protect the U.S. Later, he formed the **Department of Homeland Security**.

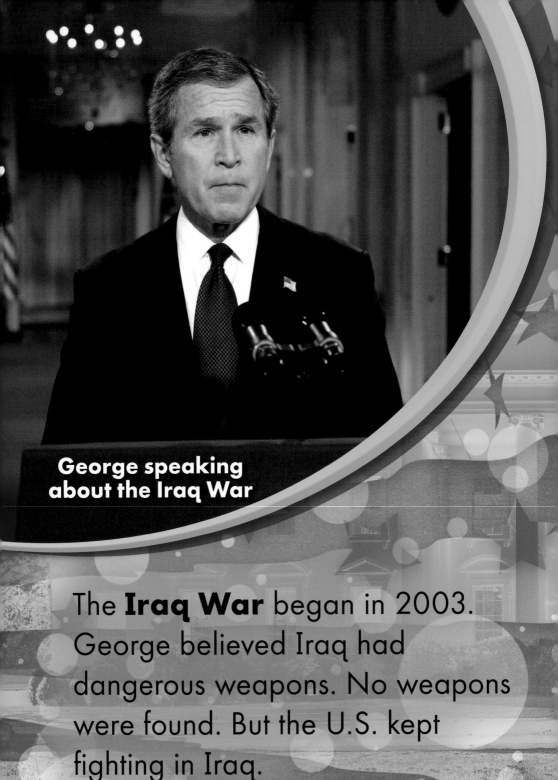

George speaking about the Iraq War

The **Iraq War** began in 2003. George believed Iraq had dangerous weapons. No weapons were found. But the U.S. kept fighting in Iraq.

George Timeline

September 11, 2001

The U.S. is attacked in what becomes known as 9/11

January 20, 2001

George W. Bush begins his presidency

October 26, 2001

George signs the Patriot Act

March 20, 2003

The Iraq War begins

August 2005

Hurricane Katrina hits the southern U.S.

January 20, 2009

George leaves office

Hurricane Katrina damage

In 2005, a big **hurricane** hit the southern U.S. People needed help. George sent aid. But it came slowly.

18

In 2007, a **recession** began.
George worked to help businesses.

What George Left Behind

George left office in 2009. As president, he faced many problems.

But he tried his best
to help the U.S.

PRESIDENT OF THE UNITED STATES · SEAL

21

Glossary

9/11—the attack on the U.S. that happened on September 11, 2001; 9/11 was the biggest attack to ever happen on U.S. soil.

Department of Homeland Security—a part of the U.S. government formed in 2002 to keep the U.S. safe from attacks

elected—chosen by voting

governor—the leader of the government of a state

graduated—finished with a course of study at a school, college, or university

hurricane—a storm formed over warm ocean waters that has fast winds and often has rain and lightning

Iraq War—a U.S.-led war fought between Iraq and many other countries that lasted from 2003 to 2011

Patriot Act—a bill passed in response to 9/11 and signed into law by President George W. Bush that changed privacy in phone and other communications

recession—a period of time in which many people do not have jobs

To Learn More

AT THE LIBRARY

Messner, Kate. *The Next President: The Unexpected Beginnings and Unwritten Future of America's Presidents.* San Francisco, Calif.: Chronicle Books, 2020.

Pettiford, Rebecca. *Barack Obama*. Minneapolis, Minn.: Bellwether Media, 2022.

Rustad, Martha E. H. *The President of the United States.* North Mankato, Minn.: Pebble, 2020.

ON THE WEB

FACTSURFER

Factsurfer.com gives you a safe, fun way to find more information.

1. Go to www.factsurfer.com.

2. Enter "George W. Bush" into the search box and click Q .

3. Select your book cover to see a list of related content.

BUSH CHENEY

Index

9/11, 5, 14

Bush, George H. W., 7

businesses, 10, 19

Connecticut, 6

Department of Homeland
   Security, 15

elected, 10, 13

Gore, Al, 12

governor, 10

Harvard, 9

hometown, 6

hurricane, 18

Iraq War, 16

Patriot Act, 15

picks, 9

profile, 13

question, 11

recession, 19

Texas, 6, 10

Texas Air National Guard, 8

timeline, 17

weapons, 16

Yale, 8